<u>Excel Tips and Tricks</u>

<u>115 Tips and Tricks</u>

<u>to increase your productivity in Excel</u>

By Vijay Kumar

Copyright © 2018

Disclaimer

Table of Contents

52. How to reduce file size

53. Copy data to new sheet to work easily

54. Use a copy of the Original workbook

55. Backup

56. Quickly enter to multiple cells

57. Fill series

58. Change Enter key direction

59. To make a chart quickly

60. Enter Data in Multiple sheets.

61. Format painter for the exact format copy

62. Find and Replace

63. Changing the look of the Excel

64. Random numbers

65. Text or Numbers

66. Changing Auto recover save interval

67. Work from left to right

68. Hide A Whole Sheet

69. Save as PDF file

70. Send an MHTML file

71. Multiple level Sorting

72. Locating all merged cells

73. Using style gallery for ready-made styles

74. Shading alternate rows (Zebra lines)

75. Monitoring the formula cells from other locations using watch window

76. Shift clicking

77. Debugging formulas

78. Cell micro-chart

79. Own Auto fill list

80. Remove grid lines

Introduction

Excel is the foremost spreadsheet program in the World. It has so many features for doing the same task. Because of this, you may end up doing things which may take some time to finish.

I have seen and rectified so many persons doing Excels work instead of doing their own work. Let Excel do the work for you rather than you doing the Excel's work.

In this book, I have compiled more than hundred tips and tricks to make you work faster in Excel.

My aim is to teach you fastest way to do things and spend less and less time in Excel doing all the unnecessary things to finish a task. You should be free to do all the important things in life as well as work.

My Assumptions about you.

I assume that you are using Excel for some time and know how to use a filter, to create a chart or pivot table or to write a formula. If you are an absolute beginner in Excel, then you should acquire basic knowledge in Excel before reading this book.

Suggestions for this book

I have taken great care in writing this book to eliminate all the errors. Still, if you find any error or if you have any suggestions for this book, please send a mail to **vijay@exceltovba.com** with the subject line Errors and Suggestions.

How to read this book?

You can read this book from top or bottom or middle, whichever way you want.

Excel Tips and Tricks

1. Alt + =

This keyboard shortcut (Alt key followed by an equal sign) will save tremendous amount of time. This one auto sums the numbers for you. Instead of typing SUM formula, you can use this shortcut to insert the formula automatically.

We will go through an example for you to understand it better. We have the data like this in the image and we want to find out the total of B, C and D columns.

	A	B	C	D
1	Name	Qnty	Rate	Total
2	Sam	1	3	3
3	Leo	5	2	10
4	Sam	1	4	4
5	Leo	5	5	25

Now select B7:D7 and then use this shortcut and press Enter. You will get the sum of three columns instantly. Before pressing Enter key check the cell range is correct. For bigger ranges, you must definitely check before pressing Enter key, if there is any empty row you will get wrong total.

Now delete the total you have just created. We will now use this shortcut in a filtered data. Filter the above data with the name Sam in the first column and then use this shortcut. Here instead of SUM formula, the SUBTOTAL formula gets inserted and you will get the total of filtered data.

So this shortcut behaves differently when you are not using the filter it uses the formula SUM, and if it is filtered, it uses the formula SUBTOTAL.

SUM will get the total of all the data irrespective of if it is filtered or not. But if you use SUBTOTAL function you will get the total of filtered data only and it is super useful.

2. Draw out equations

You can now draw equations in Excel 2016. If you have a touchscreen computer, then it is easy. Go to the Insert tab on the ribbon menu, then choose Equation > Ink Equation. You can then draw the equation in the box and then insert in Excel sheet.

3. Personal macro book

Excel will not allow you to save the macros directly in the Excel files saving with .xls or .xlsx extension due to security reasons. But you can create a personal Macro Workbook and store all macros in it. So every time you open an Excel file, Personal Macro Workbook will also get opened.

For that first open an Excel file, then click on the View tab and you can see the Macros menu at the end, and then follow these steps.

1. Select Macros – Record Macro.

2. Don't change the macro name (usually it is Macro1) and select store macro in as Personal Macro Workbook and click OK.

3. Again select Macros and click stop recording.

4. Now in the View tab click unhide and unhide the Personal.xlsb file.

5. Now got to Macros and click view macros and click edit to see the macro you have created, it begins with Sub Macro1 and ends with End Sub.

6. Again hide the Personal.xlsb file and save the Excel file and exit.

Now, this new macro will be available when you open an Excel file.

The macro you have just recorded is of no use if you have not recorded anything. But if you find any useful macros, you can include those macros in this personal book. I have given two small useful macros which you can use in the next section. One is Width column increasing macro and another one is Inserting border macro.

You can call the saved macros from the View menu > Macros > View Macros and then select and run the macro. The Personal macro book is for putting small macros so don't put big macros in there. For that, you have to create modules.

4. Inserting Borders

This one will create a border around the cell or cells you have selected. Copy from Sub to End Sub and paste it in the personal book and use it. You can assign a shortcut key also to this macro by selecting this macro from View tab > Macros > View Macros. Select the macro name and click options and assign the shortcut.

I use this shortcut key Ctrl+Shift+B.

Sub Border()

Selection.Borders.LineStyle = True

End Sub

5. Width Correction

This one will automatically adjust the width of the column according to the length of the text in the column. You can also assign a keyboard shortcut.

I use the shortcut Ctrl+Shift+W.

Sub Width_Coloumn_correction()

Cells.EntireColumn.AutoFit

Range("A1").Select

End Sub

6. Quick Access Toolbar (QAT)

You can use the Quick Access Toolbar for easy use of commands you use frequently. On the top left corner of the Excel, you can see the Toolbar. By default, there will be Save, Undo and Redo buttons. Now you can also add the functions you frequently use here, or you can add the commands which are not there in the ribbon.

Refer the image showing a small drop-down arrow to edit the QAT.

To edit the QAT click the drop-down arrow shown in the image and open up the choose More Commands and select Commands not in the Ribbon. You can add a Calculator shortcut, or a Camera or Autofilter. In this way, you can access these functions faster and save time.

7. Filter with cell content

Sometimes you want to filter the values with cell content. For that, you have to right-click the cell and use Filter by selected cells value. Instead, you can add the AutoFilter icon in the QAT as mentioned in the previous section. Now if you want to filter by cells value just select the cell and click that icon.

8. Open Excel files all at once

If you want to open two-three Excel files at once, select all the files and hit Enter.

9. Select All

This keyboard shortcut (Ctrl key followed by A) will select all the data till there is a blank row or column. And if you want to select all the data, then you have to use this shortcut once more and it will select the entire data.

10. Corner button click to select all

To select all the data in the Excel sheet you can use mouse also. Click the triangle shape in-between the first column number and first row number to select the whole sheet.

Refer the image.

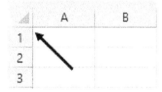

11. Increase Column width

If values inside the cell span beyond the cell length, it will not be visible. So to increase the column width, select those columns and double-click the border in between the column headings. (your cursor will change to a + sign when it reaches the border). Refer the image for you to understand.

Image before column width increasing in A, B and C columns.

Image after column width increasing

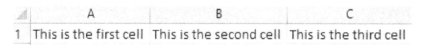

If you want to increase the width of all columns, click the corner button I have just explained in the previous section and then double-click in between the column names.

Instead of double-clicking, you can drag in between the columns after selecting the columns to get the column width of your choice.

12. Navigate between different open Excel sheets

Using the keyboard shortcut Alt + TAB to cycle through all the workbooks open and you can release the shortcut to open the workbook you have just seen.

13. Tilde character for searching * and ?

To search * and ? you can use tilde character (~), key below the escape key. * is used for searching any number of characters and ? is used to search one character at a time. So if you want to specifically search for * or ?, you have to use tilde character.

14. Copy Unique values in a column

Using Advanced filter (Data tab – Click advanced beside the Filter icon) you can copy the unique values also. Follow these steps for copying unique values.

__Refer the image__.

1. Select the cells you want the unique values from.

2. Select Advanced filter and select Copy to Location and give the starting cell range in copy to.

3. Select Unique Records and click ok and you will get the unique records.

15. Move and Copy Data in Cells

If you want to move one column of data, choose it and move (same as cut and paste) the pointer to the border. After it turns to a crossed arrow icon drag to move the column.

If you want to copy, press Ctrl button before you drag to move to a new column.

16. Enter Long Text using abbreviations

You can use Auto Correct facility for quickly entering company names in multiple parts of the sheets. Suppose you want to fill up ABC Technologies Limited when you type the abbreviation ABC.

For that, go to Excel options > Proofing and select AutoCorrect options.

In the AutoCorrect dialog box, type the text ABC in the Replace text and in the with field, you give the full company name ABC Technologies Limited. Now, whenever you type ABC, it will be replaced with the company name. Cool right.

17. Restrict data entry using Data Validation

You can use the Data validation from Data tab to restrict the data entry for simple data validations.

For example, enter the values Red, Green and Blue in the cells D1:D3. Now select A1:A10 and click the Data Validation button. Then select List from the Allow dropdown and click source and then select the source as D1:D3.

Now select A1 cell, you will get a drop down with data you have mentioned in the D1:D3. You don't have to type, select the data, and it will fill automatically.

This way you can enter data swiftly without any error.

Now, this is not a foolproof method, but to some extent, you can validate. If you copy some other data and paste it in A1 cell, then the data validation will not work.

18. Inserting Date

You can use the keyboard shortcut Ctrl followed semicolon (;) to insert today's date quickly. This saves a lot of time and the beauty is date will be inserted with the date format.

So many users enter date in the format which Excel does not recognize. This will create problems when you want to make calculations based on dates.

But using this shortcut, it will not give such headaches.

19. Data Arrangement

Whenever you save data in Excel you must store the data in a systematic way. You must keep these things in mind.

1. Data should have heading with unique names. If you are entering address spanning three columns you can use address1, address2 and address3 like that.

2. Title should be in a single cell it should not be merged

3. Column data should be of same data type, means if you are entering date all the cells in that column should contain dates

4. Don't keep any empty rows in between.

5. There should be data in each cell. If there is no data then fill it up, for text you can use any word like No data or Nil and for number use 0 (zero).

This type of data maintaining will save huge amount of time in the future if you want to make pivot reports or pivot charts or filtering.

Given below is an image of the data stored systematically.

	A	B	C	D	E	F	G
1	Location	Date	Month	Item	Price	Units Sold	Total
2	A	01-04-17	April	Ball	20	1	20
3	B	02-04-17	April	Ball	20	5	100
4	A	03-04-17	April	Glove	28	9	252
5	B	04-04-17	April	Bat	30	2	60
6	A	05-04-17	April	Glove	28	5	140
7	B	06-05-17	May	Ball	20	6	120
8	A	07-05-17	May	Ball	20	1	20
9	C	08-05-17	May	Glove	28	1	28
10	A	09-05-17	May	Bag	40	8	320
11	C	10-05-17	May	Bag	40	9	360

20. Transpose

You can change the data arrangement from vertical to horizontal or horizontal to vertical by using Transpose.

For transposing the data either you can go to Home->Paste-> and then select the transpose icon after copying the cells you want to transpose. Or else you can right click and then select transpose from paste special menu.

Refer the image, First part is before transposing and second part is after transposing.

	A	B	C	D	E	F	G	H	I
1	Single	Double		Single	1	2	3	4	5
2	1	11		Double	11	12	13	14	15
3	2	12							
4	3	13							
5	4	14							
6	5	15							

You can do the reverse transpose also.

21. Joining text values in different cells

You can use concatenate function to combine different cell values or else you can use the ampersand (&) to concatenate. For example, you have the words **This** in A1 cell, **is** in B1 and **fun** in C1. Now to combine you can use **=A1&B1&C1** and you will get **Thisisfun.**

Now if you want a space in between, you can change the formula like this **=A1&" "&B1&" "&C1.**

From Excel 2016 onwards, you can use the **TEXTJOIN** function to combine different cells values and this function is easy to use, hundred times better than using & or Concatenate function.

22. Upper, Lower and Proper functions

You can use these functions to change the text case of the letter to Upper, Lower and Proper case very fast. Don't manually change the cases by typing.

23. Values starting with zero

If you want to insert values starting with zero, use single quote and then enter the value like this **'0001.** Here the value is getting converted to text.

Or else first format the cells as text and then enter the value. This also produces the same result. If you are entering in so many cells, this will be the best option.

24. Quickly find average, count and sum

You can quickly find the Average, Count and Sum from the status bar of Excel.

For that select any bunch of numeric values and see the values magically appear in the status bar. Now right click those values to get more details like min, max values and many more.

25. Alignment of values

Usually, in Excel, the numbers are right aligned and texts are left aligned by default. Sometimes you may encounter some numbers which are aligned left and most probably it will be text.

26. Searching

If you have a big data file and if you are sure that the first column contains the data you are searching. Select that column data (means if the data is from A1:A20000 select that data) and search. This will restrict the search to that column, instead of searching the whole sheet. This will save huge amount of time.

27. Rename a sheet using double click

You can rename a sheet by double-clicking. It is much faster than right-clicking and selecting rename. Double click and enter the sheet name you want.

If you want to edit the sheet name, first double click, and then use a single click where you want to edit and make the changes.

28. Inserting a table

Use the keyboard shortcut Ctrl + T to convert the existing data into Table.

29. Name range

You can quickly name each column data if there is heading for the column.

First, select the data and select Create from Selection under Formulas tab and click ok. Make sure the Top row is ticked before clicking ok. Now the entire column headings will be the name of the range in that column.

Now you can easily subtract or multiply using the name instead of cell reference.

30. Editing the cell content

To quickly edit a cell content press the function key F2, and then edit the cell content.

31. Repeating the task

Suppose you have done a task in Excel. For example, you have changed the cell color to yellow. Now, if you select any other cell or cells and use F4 key that cell color will change to yellow. What this shortcut is doing is it imitates the previous task you have done.

So this can be used as a shortcut for so many tasks. Do the task once and then use this shortcut.

32. Save as

To quickly get the save as dialogue box you can use the function key F12.

33. Quickly add columns or rows

If you want to quickly add rows or columns, select the number of rows or columns and press Ctrl key followed by + (plus) key. Use the plus sign on the numeric pad it will be easier.

34. Quickly delete columns or rows

If you want to quickly delete rows or columns, select the number of rows or columns and press Ctrl key followed by – (minus) key. Use the minus sign on the numeric pad it will be easier.

35. Remove duplicates

To remove duplicate values, use the Remove Duplicates command on the Data tab. This one saves a lot of time.

Suppose you got a data like in this image given below and you want to remove the duplicates based on the first column.

	A	B
1	Name	Number
2	Joy	1
3	Sam	2
4	Joy	3
5	Sam	4

First, select the data you want to remove duplicates and then click on remove duplicates. Untick the heading Number from the Remove duplicates box and click ok. Keep in mind you can choose the columns based on which you can remove the duplicates and this feature is beneficial.

Image after removing duplicates based on first column

	A	B
1	Name	Number
2	Joy	1
3	Sam	2

36. Highlight duplicates

You can highlight duplicates using conditional formatting. Select the column data and select Conditional Formatting from the Home tab. Select Highlight Cells Rule > Duplicate values and click ok. The Duplicate values will be highlighted. You have the option to choose the color before clicking ok.

37. Finding the number of duplicates

Using Conditional formatting, we have learned how to highlight the duplicate value. What if we want to know the first, second, or third duplicate value in a column? For that, you can use the **COUNTIF** function.

	A	B	C
1	Name	Duplicate	Formula used
2	Joy	1	COUNTIF($A$2:A2,A2)
3	Sam	1	COUNTIF($A$2:A3,A3)
4	Joy	2	COUNTIF($A$2:A4,A4)
5	Mily	1	COUNTIF($A$2:A5,A5)
6	Sam	2	COUNTIF($A$2:A6,A6)
7	Lucy	1	COUNTIF($A$2:A7,A7)
8	Joy	3	COUNTIF($A$2:A8,A8)

In the image, you can see the name Joy occurred three times and Sam occurred two times. In the formula first parameter you have to type the range you want to search and second parameter you give the criteria.

We have locked the first parameters first cell A2 using dollar so that the search will always start from A2. Now when you copy down the formula, COUNTIF will count the occurrence of the value mentioned in the second parameter.

38. Hide individual cells

You can hide cell contents using this trick. Right-click a cell and select choose Format Cells and set the format as Custom under the Number tab. Enter ;;; (three semicolons) as the format. The cell contents disappear, but they're still there and can be used in formulas.

39. HIDE/UNHIDE ROWS

Sometimes, you may want to hide some rows or columns of data. This can be for printing or for hiding the data from the audience if it is a presentation or if there are so many columns.

Right-click the row or columns you want to hide and then select Hide. You can use these shortcuts also if you want.

CTRL key followed by 9 to hide the selected Rows.

CTRL key followed by 0 to hide the selected Columns.

40. Group or Ungroup Rows or Columns

By using Row and Column groupings, you can quickly hide and unhide columns and rows.

First, select the rows or columns you want to group and then click Group from Data tab > Group. You can make different groups by selecting different rows or columns.

Shift+Alt+Right Arrow is the shortcut to group rows or columns.

Shift+Alt+Left Arrow is the shortcut to ungroup. This is the same as pressing the Clear Outline button on the Ungroup menu of the Data tab.

See the image below; I have grouped the rows and columns. By clicking the minus sign, you can easily collapse the rows and columns.

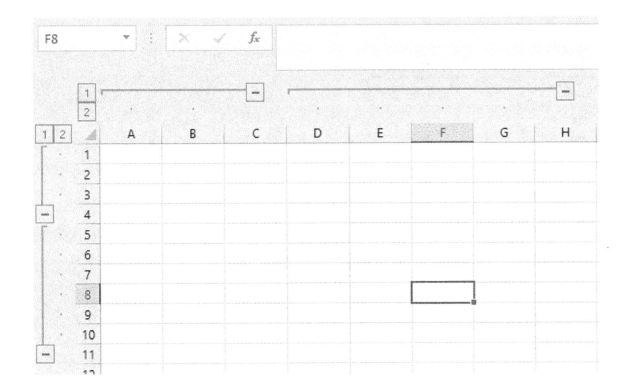

41. Flash fill

Flash fill is a new feature introduced in Excel 2013 and saves enormous amount of time. If you're reformatting data in an adjacent column, Flash Fill will recognize patterns and fill out the rest of the details for you.

Image before flash fill

	A	B
1	First name	Second name
2	Joy	Thomas
3	Sam	Alexander
4	Lucy	Philip
5	Mily	Roger

Here we are combining the two names. First, you enter the combined name Joy Thomas in C2 cell. Next type the names first letter and Flash fill will give you the suggestion and then press Enter. You will get full name in all the columns.

Image during the flash fill.

	A	B	C
1	First name	Second name	Full name
2	Joy	Thomas	Joy Thomas
3	Sam	Alexander	Sam Alexander
4	Lucy	Philip	Lucy Philip
5	Mily	Roger	Mily Roger

42. Copy down above cell details.

Use the keyboard shortcut **Ctrl followed by D** to copy the above cell content to below cells. First, select the cell content you want to copy along with the cells you want to paste and then use this shortcut.

43. Largest number in-between

Sometimes you want to find out the second largest number or third largest number. In this case, you can use the Large function.

You can use the formula like this **=LARGE(range,n)**. n denotes the number you want to specify second largest or third or which order you want.

44. Smallest number in-between

Similarly, you can find the smallest values in between by using the SMALL function.

45. Remove unnecessary spaces

You can use the TRIM function to remove leading and trailing spaces except for single spaces between the words if you are using it in a sentence.

For Example, if you use this on Hello World, you will get the same words. But if you use it on **Hello World,** then it will be trimmed to **Hello World**.

46. Counting of cells

COUNT() function only counts number of cells with numbers in them. But COUNTA() function will count all the cells irrespective of text or numbers mentioned. And COUNTBLANK will count only blank cells in the range.

Refer the image below to understand this better.

	A	B
1	1	
2	HI	
3	&	
4		
5	4	
6	5	
7		
8	**Answer**	**Formula used**
9	3	COUNT(A1:A6)
10	5	COUNTA(A1:A6)
11	1	COUNTBLANK(A1:A6)

Count doesn't consider HI and & symbol. But Counta considered these and Countblank counted only the blank cells in the range.

47. Disable annoying formula errors

To disable annoying formula error go to Excel options > Formulas > Error Checking rules and disable errors you don't want to see.

48. See all formulas at once

Sometimes you want to see all the formulas you have entered in Excel sheet. Use keyboard shortcut Ctrl and the acute accent key (`), below the Esc key on the left corner. You will see all the formulas instead of their values.

Use this shortcut once more to go back to the previous state.

49. Finding formulas

There are so many formulas in Excel. So if you don't know the name of a particular formula to use for a particular purpose you can search that formula. For that in Formulas tab click Insert function and type the formula you want to search. For example, if you don't know any lookup formulas, type lookup and then click Go.

You will get the list of functions related to lookup. From this, you will get some idea about the formula.

50. Refreshing the Pivot table

The pivot table will not refresh automatically if fresh data is added. So you have to click refresh after selecting the pivot table.

Now if you want to update the pivot table automatically change the data sheet to table. All the new data will be refreshed automatically in Pivot table.

You have the option to refresh the pivot on opening the file. For that, select the option Refresh data when opening the file under Data tab in PivotTable Options.

51. Copy or Move a Worksheet to different Workbook

Open two saved workbooks with some data in the sheets. Now select any book and right click on the sheet name you want to copy and select Move or Copy to. If the name is not changed it will be Sheet1 or Sheet2 or Sheet3.

Select the sheet name you want a copy and then check the Create a copy and select the workbook name you want to copy to.

For moving the sheet don't check the Create a copy check box.

52. How to reduce file size

1. **Remove formatting from empty rows and columns.**

   Select the range which you do not need any formatting and goto Home Tab > Editing Group > Clear > Clear Formats.

2. **Remove any unused cells**

   Sometimes you have the actual data upto cell E30. But Excel is considering the last used cell as E20000. Now this will increase the file size. So first find the last cell by using the shortcut CTRL+END. Then select all the cells from thirty-first to twenty thousand row and delete the entire rows. You file size will be reduced.

3. **Remove unnecessary Graphics**

   Remove Graphics that are not needed as they take huge space.

4. **Compress Image**

   If you have so many images in the spreadsheet, compress each picture in your spreadsheet. When you click the image, you will get a Tab called Format. In that, you have the option called Compress pictures to compress the image.

5. **Using Entire Column/Row Range in Formulas.**

   Don't use the entire columns and rows in the formulas, like SUM(H:H) or AVERAGE(2:2). Instead, use the row number and column number till the data is there.

   Also, limit the use of Array formulas as it will use space and slow down the Excel.

6. **Conditional Formatting**

   Use Conditional formatting sparingly and apply to the only cell range you wanted. Don't apply to whole columns.

7. **Query Tables**

   After using query table to get data, disconnect the table or acquire the data and delete the query table.

8. **Zip the Excel file**

   You can use any compressing software to zip the file and it will reduce the file size to ninety percent if there is no image.

9. **Save the Excel file in .xlsb File Format**

   Also, you can save the file in xlsb is Binary File Format. This type of file can have Macros in it unlike xlsx file format and works faster than any other excel file format.

10. **Value paste formulas**

    If you have so many lookup formulas (Vlookup or Hlookup) in an Excel file, the file size will increase. So to reduce the file size, you can paste all the formulas as values. This will reduce the file size considerably.

53. Copy data to new sheet to work easily

If the data you have is so big, it will take so much time to delete the unwanted data after filtering. Instead, filter the data you want and then copy that data to a new sheet and then work on it.

54. Use a copy of the Original workbook

If you are working on big data file which has important information. First, make a copy of the file and work on that.

55. Backup

Instead of losing critical data in Excel it is always safe to backup the Excel sheet to other network drive or use cloud storage like Dropbox or Google drive.

56. Quickly enter to multiple cells

If you want to quickly enter the values to multiple cells, use the keyboard shortcut Ctrl followed by Enter key. For example, select a range and enter 25 and press Ctrl + Enter. 25 will be pasted in the range you have selected.

57. Fill series

To fill a series fast, enter the first two values one by one in the same column and the select those two values. Move the cursor to the right hand lower end till the cursor is changed to a black plus sign. Now click and drag till the row you want to fill the series.

If there is data in the previous column, you can double-click the black plus sign. This will be fast. Data will be filled down in the current column to the rows filled in the previous column.

58. Change Enter key direction

In Excel, if you press Enter key, it will go to the next cell below. You can change the direction of the Enter key.

Go to Excel options > Advanced > Editing options and change **After pressing Entermove selection**.

59. To make a chart quickly

To make a chart quickly, press the keyboard shortcut F11.

60. Enter Data in Multiple sheets.

If you want to enter formula or data in multiple sheets at once. First, select all the sheets and then enter the formula or data. You will have the same details on all the sheets.

This is useful if someone is maintaining month wise expense in different sheets. The data will be different but if you are entering the same formula select all the sheet and enter the formula in first sheet, the same formula will be there in all sheets.

61. Format painter for the exact format copy

Select a cell you want to copy the format from and then click the format painter button and then apply the format to another cell by clicking that cell. Format painter can be selected from Home tab.

Refer the screen shot below highlighting the Format Painter.

If you want to apply the format to multiple cells, double-click the format painter and then apply to multiple cells.

62. Find and Replace

You can use Find and Replace to clean up the data instantly. Suppose a particular range has an opening bracket in between the texts and you want to remove this bracket.

Use the keyboard shortcut Ctrl + H to get Find and Replace window. You can put the opening bracket in the Find What and then don't put anything in the Replace with, and then click Replace all to remove the bracket.

If you want to remove in particular cells or column, then select those cells or columns and do this.

63. Changing the look of the Excel

You can change the look of the Excel. For that go to File > Options > General and change the Office theme (in Excel 2013 and 2016), change the Color Scheme Excel 2010 and 2007.

64. Random numbers

If you want to populate a bunch of cells with numbers instantly, you can use the RAND or RANDBETWEEN functions.

Rand function will give decimal numbers between 0 and 1. So if you want decimal numbers above one you can multiply the Rand function with ten or hundred or thousand as per your requirement.

Randbetween you can specify the numbers in between you want, like this =RANDBETWEEN(10,200). This will generate random numbers between 10 and 200.

65. Text or Numbers

If you see some numbers in a range and to quickly find if it is text or number. Select them and check whether it is showing sum or count in status bar. If it is number, it will show sum and if it is text, it will show count.

66. Changing Auto recover save interval

Excel has an AutoRecover feature which automatically saves changes if the file has already been saved at least once. The default value is ten minutes. You can shorten or lengthen this interval. You should change this to two minutes so you don't have to save the file in-between.

For that, go to Excel Options and click the Save tab and the Save options appear in the right pane.

Use the spinner buttons or enter a new automatic save interval into the Save AutoRecover Information Every xx Minutes text box.

Click OK to close the Excel Options dialog box.

67. Work from left to right

Always put the data on the left side of the Excel and formulas on the right side. By default, Excel calculates at the top-left corner of the sheet first and then continues to the right and down.

In big sheets with thousands of rows, calculations will be faster when you put the data on the left side and the formulas on the right.

68. Hide A Whole Sheet

You can hide an Excel sheet by right-clicking the sheet and select hide to hide the details from other persons. But if the other person knows there is a hidden sheet he can right-click the sheet name and select unhide.

Here is another technique you can use to really hide the sheet.

Open Excel and use the keyboard shortcut Alt + F11 to open Visual Basic Editor.

In the Project Explorer select sheet3, you want to hide.(If Project Explorer is not visible select view project Explorer).

In the Properties window (select properties window from view menu if it is not visible) select the change the visible property to **2 – xlS etVeryHidden** from the Visible property's drop-down list.

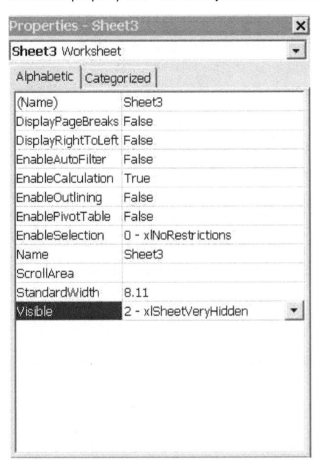

When you change this property Excel selects the first sheet, Sheet1 after hiding the third sheet. It is a normal behavior; you can again select the sheet3 and see the visible property is applied.

Now if you go back to Excel sheet, sheet3 will not be visible and will not be there in the Unhide dialog box. The average user won't know the sheet exists, let alone know how to unhide it. But the person who knows VBA can unhide the sheet.

To unhide Sheet3, return to the VBE and choose -1 - xlSheetVisible.

69. Save as PDF file

You can save the Excel as PDF file. Click save as and select the file type as PDF. In Earlier version before 2007, you have to make use of any third-party PDF generator.

70. Send an MHTML file

If you want to send someone the details of the report you have made. You can send the same as MTHML file and for opening this file only browser is needed. Click save as and select the file type webpage with mhtml extension.

71. Multiple level Sorting

Usually, you sort any one of the columns. But you can also sort multiple levels. This allows you to sort your data by more than one column.

Click the Data tab, select the Sort command. Click Add Level to add another column to sort by.

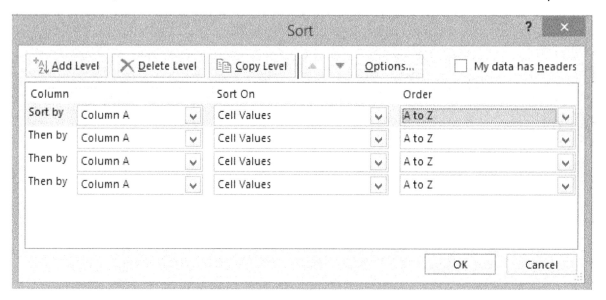

The worksheet will be sorted according to the selected order. If there are numbers, you can sort from smallest to larges. If it is text, it will be sorted alphabetically.

If you need to change which column should be sorted first. Simply select the desired column, and then click the Move Up or Move Down arrow to adjust its priority.

72. Locating all merged cells

You can find all the merged cells in your worksheet with the Find command and then unmerge those cells.

First, select the range and press Ctrl+F from the keyboard to open excel Find window.

Click the Options button, and then the Format button.

After clicking on the format button, Find Format window will open, navigate to the Alignment Tab.

Uncheck the Wrap Text and Shrink to Fit options. Check the Merge Cells Option and click OK.

Now click the Find All button, this will show you all the merged cells present in the specified range.

73. Using style gallery for ready-made styles

You can quickly format a cell by choosing a cell style. For this select Cell Styles under Home tab and use the style you want.

You can also create your own cell style. For this follow these steps.

1. On the Home tab, in the Styles group, click the bottom right down arrow and select New Cell Style.

2. Enter a name and click the Format button to define the Number Format, Alignment, Font, Border, Fill and Protection of your cell style. After selecting the format click OK.

3. Now the new style created will be available in Cell Styles under Custom.

You can also delete or modify the cell style created. For that, Right-click a cell style to modify or delete it.

Modifying a cell style affects all cells in a workbook that use that cell style. This can save a lot of time as you have to edit in only one place.

A cell style is stored in the workbook where you create it. So if you want to import a cell style to another workbook. Open a new workbook and click on Merge Styles (under New Cell Style) to import a cell style. You should open the workbook with the cell style top copy the style.

74. Shading alternate rows (Zebra lines)

For better readability of data, you can shade alternate rows and the easiest way is to change the data to table. For this select the data and use the shortcut Ctrl + T or navigate to the Insert tab and click Table. You can select different Table styles from the Design Tab to change the look.

Now, this data is converted to table and if you don't want the table functionality, you can easily convert the table back to a usual range. To do this, select any cell within your table, right click and choose Convert to Range from the context menu.

If you opt to convert a table to a range, you won't get the zebra lines when you add new rows to the range.

Another disadvantage is if you move, delete or sort the data shading will not look like Zebra line. In this case, remove the formatting an again create the table, it is that simple.

75. Monitoring the formula cells from other locations using watch window

If your data spans hundreds or thousands of rows, it will be difficult to watch the cells at different parts of the sheet. You can use Watch Window for this purpose.

Watch Window will give information about the cells in a separate window and keep track of them there. This saves you from having to scroll all over your worksheet.

Click on the Formulas tab and click Watch Window under the Formula Auditing section. In the Add Watch dialogue box, either type the cell reference directly or select the cells with the mouse.

Also, you can add contiguous cells to the Watch Window by clicking and dragging your mouse to select a series of cells. When you are done, click on the Add button. Now if any changes happen to the watching cell or cells will immediately show up in the Watch Window.

Secondly, the Watch Window also reports other important information about cells. It gives information about the workbook and worksheet in which the cells reside and the name of the cell, formulas etc.

You can drag the Watch Window to one of the sides of Excel to dock it so that it doesn't take up valuable space on the worksheet floating around.

In Watch window you can add cells from other sheets within the same Excel workbook, but you can't add cells from another workbook. Each workbook has its own separate Watch Window.

If you work with large spreadsheets, Watch Window is a real time saver and is likely to increase your productivity. It allows you to spend more time on your work and less time clicking around in Excel.

76. Shift clicking

You can use SHIFT key with left mouse click to click the range of cells. First, select the cell and then use SHIFT and left click to select the whole cells in between. Instead, you can use a cell and drag to the cell you want to select the cell range.

77. Debugging formulas

If you have a big formula and want to see what is each portion of the formula is returning, select the portions of formula from formula bar and press F9 you will see that portions result.

78. Cell micro-chart

To quickly insert a micro-chart inside a cell, use the REPT() function. This will repeat the number of characters you specify.

	A	B	C
1	No.	Chart	Formula used
2	2	II	REPT("I",A1)
3	3	III	REPT("I",A2)
4	6	IIIIII	REPT("I",A3)
5	9	IIIIIIIII	REPT("I",A4)
6	1	I	REPT("I",A5)
7	10	IIIIIIIIII	REPT("I",A6)
8	20	IIIIIIIIIIIIIIIIIIII	REPT("I",A7)

Here in the image, I have repeated the letter I the number of times with the number mentioned in the A column.

79. Own Auto fill list

You might have noticed an Auto fill feature in Excel, For Example, if you enter Jan in A1 cell, Feb in A2 cell and then select those two cells and drag the cells from the bottom right-hand corner cell (your cursor will turn to a black plus sign the only you should drag)to the bottom cells the cells will be filled with Mar, April, May so on. Like this, you can also make you own Auto fill list.

Go to Excel options and select Advanced > General > Edit Custom Lists. In the custom list, you can add your own list and click add. Now next time if you add the first text in the list and drag down you will get the list filled up with the custom list created by you.

80. Remove grid lines

You can remove grid lines from the excel worksheet. For this go to menu > tools > options > and un-check gridlines option.

81. Select all formulas

To select all the formulas in the Excel sheet, press CTRL+G, select special and check formula. You can then format the formulas by giving color or make it bold.

82. Select all constants

To select all the constants in the Excel sheet, press CTRL+G, select special and check constants. You can then format the constants by giving color or make it bold.

83. Save newly created charts as templates

When you have created a chart using various combinations and wanted to use it later, you can save it save it as a template so you can use it again. Right-click on the chart created and select Save as Template.

By default, these charts are saved in Charts folder. All templates stored in this folder are automatically added to the Templates folder that appears in the Insert Chart and Change Chart Type dialogs when you create a new or modify an existing graph in Excel. Templates saved in Charts folder appear in the Templates folder in Excel. So don't change the default destination folder when saving a template.

If you want to make use of any chart templates downloaded from the Internet, save those files in the Chart folder. Usually, this is the default location of the chart.

C:\Users\User_name\AppData\Roaming\Microsoft\Templates\Charts

If the above path is not working, then right-click the Save as Template from the Excel and you can see the folder there.

How to apply the chart template

If you want to apply the saved template, open the Insert Chart dialog by clicking the Dialog Box Launcher in the Charts group on the ribbon. On the All Charts tab, switch to the Templates folder, and click on the template you want to apply.

84. Splitting the sentence inside a cell

If you want to split a sentence inside a cell, place the cursor before the text you want to split inside the cell and then use Alt + Enter.

Before splitting image

After splitting the image by putting the cursor before the word before

85. Create image from a range

You can create an image of cell range and use it in Excel sheet. First, select the range and copy the range. Then right click and select paste special and select other paste options and then select Picture. You will get a picture of the range. Now you can format this picture by right-clicking the picture and selecting format shape.

86. Create a live image of a range

Also, you can make a live image of the range also. Instead of selecting Picture in Paste special you must select Linked Picture. So whenever any changes happen to the range the image content will also change accordingly.

In this case, also you can format the image created.

87. Saving range as GIF or Jpeg

The easiest way to save the range as Gif or Jpeg is to use the snipping tool in windows. Select the snipping tool and select the area you want to save and then snipping tool will extract the selection and you can save it as Gif or Jpeg or Png.

If the snipping tool is not available, then you have to use the Paint or any other image editing software. First, click print screen from the keyboard and then paste in the image editing software and then save it.

88. Select Entire rows or columns

If you want to select an entire column in a sheet you can use the keyboard shortcut Ctrl + Spacebar. For selecting an entire row, you can use Shift + Spacebar.

89. Freeze Panes

If you have so many rows of data and row headings will not be visible if you scroll down. In this case, you can use Freeze Top Row from Freeze Panes in View tab. Now if you scroll down, you can see the row heading.

90. Create tables in Excel

If you are working with big data in Excel, it is better to change the data to tables. This will make your life easier.

You can use the shortcut Ctrl + T to convert the entire data to table or select Insert tab and then click Table. Select the data range and click ok. Tables have these benefits

Drop-Down Filters

Tables have dropdown filters in each column which allow you to filter your data.

Column Headings are Always Visible

When you scroll down your data and the row with your column headers won't disappear it will be visible all the time. If you are outside the table, this won't work. You should be inside the table for this to work.

Automatic Calculation on your data

You have an option in Excel table to add sum or min or max or average. For that check the option Total Row in the Design tab. If it is not visible click the table and you will see the Design tab.

Once the Total Row is ticked, you will get a total column at the bottom. The beauty of this is you will get totals based on the filter you select. And second thing if you click the total amount you can change the same to Sum or Average. This you can do for individual columns. For one column you can set the total and another column you can set average.

Banded Rows

You have noticed that every other row in table is shaded. This will make the data easier to read. This shading is automatically applied. Also, you can select a different color scheme, choose another Table Style from the gallery.

Dynamic Named Range

Excel table will automatically expand when you add a new record, even if it is added at the end of the table. So the range of cells that your name refers to will also automatically expand. This is known as a dynamic range.

To add a new record to an Excel Table, click into the last cell of the last record (above your Total Row if you are displaying it) and then press the TAB key on your keyboard. This creates a new blank row and becomes a part of the table. This is true for column also when it is added it becomes the part of the table.

Magic Formulas

Instead of displaying a cell address table will refer the range with the table heading. So it will be easy to type a formula. By just looking at the formula you will know which columns are used because of using the column header names.

Also if you enter a formula in one cell, it automatically gets copies to rest of the column.

Create a Dynamic Range of Charts & PivotTables

Excel Tables create a dynamic range. So if you are creating pivot table or charts, it will be automatically updated to show the new data.

91. Convert Formulas to Values

If you have so many formulas in an Excel sheet convert the formulas to values. This will speed up the calculation time in Excel. If you use Vlookup, then change the Vlookup formula to values.

92. Volatile functions

Don't use or minimize using the volatile function NOW, TODAY, INDIRECT, RAND, OFFSET. These functions will recalculate each time when any other cell values are changed and this will in turn slow down the Excel considerably. If the data set is bigger then I would recommend don't use it.

93. Don't use the Entire Row/Column as Reference (A:A)

Never use the full column reference in the formulas. For example, if you have the data till twenty thousand row and you are using the full column reference, it will search the whole column till the end of the row.

This will slow down the Excel very much.

94. Manual Calculation Mode

If your Excel file is big and has so many formulas, then it will slow down the Excel each time any value changes. So when you are writing formulas change it to manual mode and once you complete entering formula you can change back to automatic. To change to manual mode, go to Formula Tab –> Calculation Options –> Manual. Once you make any changes press F9 key to recalculate if you want.

You can change back to automatic once the formulas are entered. Keep in mind if you don't change back and if you change any figures, the formulas will not get updated and will give wrong results. Especially true if you are reopening that same file after one week and you forget it is in manual or automatic.

95. Use -- (double negatives) to convert TRUE and FALSE

If you want the logical function in Excel to give the result as either "1" or "0" instead of "TRUE" or "FALSE," simply use double minus signs as part of your formula.

So if you are using a large dataset, it will speed up the calculations.

For Example, if you type **=(10>5),** you will get the answer True. But if you put two negative signs like this **=--(10>5)** it will give the answer 1. In computer terms 1 is true and 0 is false. Now you can use this 1 and 0 in formulas directly as True and False cannot be used in a formula.

96. Use the INDEX/MATCH instead of VLOOKUP

If you are using Vlookup in an Excel sheet in lot of columns with huge data set it will definitely slow down the Excel. It is better switch to Index/Match to speed up the Excel.

97. Select and Populate Blank Cells

First, select the entire data set and press F5 to open the Go To dialogue box.

Click on Special button top open Go To Special dialogue box and then select the Blanks radio button.

This selects all the blank cells in your data set. Now you can enter zero or the text of your choice in all these cells. Type it and press Control + Enter to enter the value is all the cells. If you press Enter, the value is inserted only in the active cell.

98. Clear Formatting

To clear the formats given to the cells. Select data and Go to Home –> Clear –> Clear Formats. This will clear all the formats.

99. Highlight Formulas Errors – One way

Select the entire data set and Go to Home –> Conditional Formatting –> New Rule

In New Formatting Rule Dialogue Box select 'Format Only Cells that Contain'

In the Rule Description, select Errors from the drop down

Set the format and give a color and click OK. This highlights any error value in the selected dataset

100. Highlight Formula Errors – Another way

First, select the entire data set and press F5 to open the Go To Dialogue box.

Click on Special Button at the bottom left

Select Formulas and uncheck all options except Errors

This selects all the cells that have an error in it. Now you can manually highlight with color or delete or type a text etc.

101. Quickly Enter Numbers with Fixed Decimal Numbers

If you want to speed up entering data that has a decimal part to it, then this will be useful. You can type the numbers without hitting the dot key every time. For example, you have to enter numbers with up to two decimal points. You can enable this feature from Excel options.

In the Excel Options Dialogue box, select Advanced.

In Advanced Options, Under editing options check the option, Automatically Insert a decimal point.

Specify the number of decimals you want (for example 2 in this case).

Now, whenever you enter any number, excel automatically places last two digits after the decimal. So 2 becomes .02, 20 becomes 0.2, 200 becomes 2, 8935 becomes 89.35 and so on.

102. Enter current time

You can enter the current time very fast using this keyboard shortcut Control + Shift + : (colon key)

103. Alt + Down Arrow (Keyboard shortcut)

This shortcut is very useful.

There are three uses for this shortcut

1. You can speed up the repetitive data entry accurately within a column

For example, you have the word Apple in A1, Orange in A2 cell, Mango in A3 and Apple in A4 cell. Now use this shortcut in the A5 cell you will sell all the unique texts entered in the column. Now you can select the text you want from this alphabetical order list. Use the down arrow key to select the text and press Enter. This way it will increase the accuracy and data capturing speed.

Refer the image given below to understand.

This can be done only just below the cell having the data. It will not work if you are using this shortcut in the same column deep down the column without having the data in the just above cell.

2. The second thing is once you have filtered the data you can use this shortcut to access the filtering menu without using the mouse.

Filtered data.

	A
1	Fruits ▼
2	Apple
3	Orange
4	Mango
5	Apple

After using the shortcut.

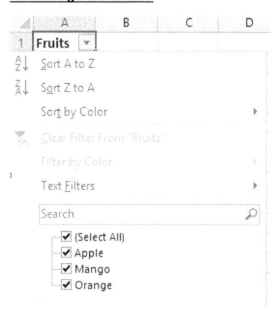

3. Third, you can use to select an option from Data Validation lists without using the mouse

104. Navigate through multiple worksheets

You can use the keyboard shortcut Control + Page Up/Page Down to navigate through different sheets in the excel sheet. This is much faster than selecting the sheets using a mouse. If you have more than sheets then this one is very useful.

Control + Page Up is used to go to the previous sheet.

Control + Page Down is used to go to next sheet.

105. Take Screenshots in Excel

You can capture snapshots of programs or windows that you have open on your computer.

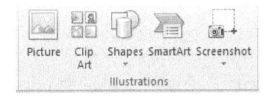

Select Insert tab and click the Screenshot button. Open program windows are displayed as thumbnails. You can insert the whole window or select part of a window. Only windows that have not been minimized to the taskbar can be captured.

106. Save time by creating a Workspace

If you open the same group of Excel workbooks every day, you can save yourself some time by creating a workspace.

Instead of opening these files one by one you can save them as workspace and click on that file. All the files related the workspace will open immediately. For this follow this steps.

Open all the workbooks you want to save as a group and click the View tab.

Click Save Workspace in the Window group, enter a name for the group, and click Save. Your workspace will be saved with xlw extension

To open all the workbooks in the group, double-click the file with xlw extension you have just created.

Your workbooks are still separate files. You can open and close them individually, as you normally would.

This feature is discontinued from Excel 2013.

107. Watch formula evaluated step by step (for Windows only)

If you want to see how a complicated formula is been solved step by step. Go to Formulas > Evaluate Formula to see the calculations run step by step.

108. Import data from the Web

If you want to use any well formatted HTML table from Web you can use this trick. If it is poorly formatted also you will be able to get the data.

For this go to Data tab > New Query > From Other Sources > From Web in Excel 2016. Enter the URL of the Web page and you will get HTML tables on that page. Click on a table to see a preview; when you find the one you want, click Load.

For Excel 2010 or 2013 you have to install the Power query addin to use this feature and you will get a separate Tab called Power Query. From this tab you can click the From tab and give the URL.

The great thing is if the data changes in the actual webpage you can refresh the data by right-clicking the table.

109. Custom Excel number format

Excel has a lot of built-in formats for number, percentage, dates etc. But if you don't find any format according to your need you can create a custom format.

To create a custom Excel format select a cell for which you want to create custom formatting, and press Ctrl+1 to open the Format Cells dialog or right click and select Format cells.

Instead of creating a custom number format from scratch, you choose a built-in Excel format close to your desired result, and customize it.

110. Define Constants

You can define a constant in Excel if you want. For example, if the loan rate is 12% then you can define this as a constant and use this in the calculation instead of multiplying it directly. The beauty is if the rate changes next year edit the constant and in rest of the sheets it will be applied automatically.

To make a constant, go to Formulas tab and click Define Name. Put a name and the value in the bottom box. Now you can use this constant anywhere in the Excel sheet.

If you want to edit the constant value go to Name manager in Formula tab and edit.

111. Quickly insert a dollar sign

By using the function key F4 you can quickly insert the dollar sign for changing the cell reference to Mixed or Absolute while entering the formulas. You can keep hitting the F4 key to change the reference. When you are using Vlookup or Index Match formulas this will become handy.

112. Insert currency format

To apply the currency format quickly to a range, use the shortcut Ctrl+Shift+$. This will apply the default currency format to the range.

113. Copy cells from left side to right hand side

Use the keyboard shortcut **Ctrl followed by R** to copy the left hand side column content to current column or right hand column cells. First, select the cell content you want to copy along with the cells you want to paste to the right and then use this shortcut.

114. Paste

To paste the values you have cut or copied use the Enter key.

115. Learn Excel programming

This is not a tip or trick in Excel. But learning VBA (Visual Basic for Application) programming in Excel is the most time saver and productive tool in Excel. This will save huge amount of time for you. All the above tips and tricks and the combinations can be done with VBA in seconds. So spend some amount of time every day and learn VBA.

Conclusion

Hope you have enjoyed my book Excel Tips and Tricks. If you have enjoyed this book and found it useful, please write a review of this book on Amazon.

I go through the reviews seriously and always go through them to improve my book and myself. By giving reviews, you are helping me provide better content that you will love in the future. A review doesn't have to be long, just one or two sentences and a number of stars you find appropriate (hopefully 5 of course). Also, if I think your review is useful, I will mark it as 'helpful'.

Once again thank you for reading this book.

About the Author

Hi, my name is Vijay Kumar and I 'am crazy about learning as well as teaching Excel. This book is a compilation of the knowledge I have acquired by teaching as well learning Excel from the past twelve years.

My Other Books

1. Excel Shortcuts: 130 Shortcuts that will change your life forever

This book covers various shortcuts from Basic to Advance level in Formatting, Data editing, Selection, Navigation and other useful shortcuts with examples.

These are some of the benefits of learning Shortcuts.

• Increase your productivity by speeder execution of tasks.
• Will increase the accuracy of the work you are doing.
• Help to get Raises and Promotion.
• To impress your Boss and Colleagues.
• It is fun to use the shortcuts.

2. Excel Formulas: 140 Excel Formulas and Functions with usage and examples

Do you want to know more about the Excel Formulas then this book is for you?

This book provides more than 140 Formulas and there uses with example workbook for you to understand and use it in your day to day work.

3. Vlookup Mastery: Learn Vlookup Hlookup and Index Match In-Depth

This book is specifically written for the lookups function in Excel. This book covers advanced concepts in Vlookup, Hlookup and Index Match functions.

If you know these three functions in depth, then all the database capabilities of the Excel can be utilized to its fullest capability.

Each chapter contains example files for you to practice along while you read this book. By implementing the techniques specified in this book you will save a huge amount of time.

All the example files are explained in detail with simple data.

I can definitely say this book will address so many problems you face with the Lookup functions.

4. Excel Macros: VBA Programming for Beginners

Excel is the number one Spreadsheet Application in the World. Almost all the Excel users know how to write formulas, formatting or creating a pivot table. But they don't know how to automate these tasks. With the help of Excel Macros, you can automate all the repetitive task while you relax in your chair.

This book is for those who have no programming knowledge and want to learn writing macros. If you want Excel work for you rather than you work for Excel, then this book is for you.

This book has more than 190 simple examples to understand the basics of VBA programming language for writing Macros. .

This book covers all the necessary knowledge required for creating macros.

The main portions covered in the book are.

What is VBA?

Visual Basic Editor (VBE)

Excel Object Model, Procedures and Functions

Elements of VBA Language

Range Object

Built-In VBA Functions

Operators in Excel VBA

Controlling Program Flow and Making Decisions

Error Handling

Debugging the Codes

Add-Ins creation in Excel

So once you complete reading this book, you can start writing macros on your own.

www.ingramcontent.com/pod-product-compliance
Lightning Source LLC
LaVergne TN
LVHW081701050326
832903LV00026B/1863